✦ Winnie-the-Pooh's COOKIE BOOK ✦

✦ *Inspired by* **A. A. MILNE** ✦

Winnie·the·Pooh's
COOKIE BOOK

With Decorations by **ERNEST H. SHEPARD**

DUTTON BOOKS · NEW YORK

Library of Congress Cataloging-in-Publication Data
Winnie-the-Pooh's cookie book / inspired by A. A. Milne, with decorations by
Ernest H. Shepard. p. cm. *Summary*: More than forty recipes feature vignettes of the
Milne characters. ISBN 0-525-45688-0 (hardcover) 1. Cookies—Juvenile literature.
[1. Cookies. 2. Cookery. 3. Literary cookbooks.] I. Milne, A. A. (Alan Alexander),
1882-1956. II. Shepard, Ernest H. (Ernest Howard), 1879-1976.
TX772.W53 1996 641.8'654—dc20 96-20783 CIP AC
Published in the United States 1996 by
Dutton Books, a division of Penguin Books USA Inc.
375 Hudson Street, New York, New York 10014
Printed in Hong Kong
Written by Dawn Martin

CONTENTS

A WORD ABOUT COOKIES

"When you wake up in the morning, Pooh," said Piglet at last, "what's the first thing you say to yourself?"

"What's for breakfast?" said Pooh. "What do you say, Piglet?"

"I say, I wonder what's going to happen exciting today?" said Piglet.

Pooh nodded thoughtfully.

"It's the same thing," he said. —Winnie-the-Pooh

Thick or thin, soft or crisp, dropped or rolled or shaped or sliced, cookies mean happiness. The following recipes include some cookies that are perfect *anytime,* ideal for lunch-box treats or after-school snacks. There are also cookies especially for *company,* with extra-special ingredients to make them extra-specially delicious. *Honey-Pot* cookies are cookies made with honey—so moist and delectable, they might never get any further than Pooh! And finally, there are cookies for the *holidays,* to help make those joyous occasions even more festive.

The following recipes are simple and fun to make, but some doughs need to be refrigerated, so be sure to plan ahead and leave enough time. Once baked, allow the cookies to cool, then decorate using colored icing, sparkling sugar, melted chocolate, or simply powdered sugar. And don't forget the rules of kitchen safety. Young cooks should have adult supervision when working with the stove or oven.

Cookie Wisdom

+ 1 BAKING: Always preheat the oven before baking. And since cookies spread while baking, be sure to leave at least 2 inches between them on the cookie sheets.
+ 2 ROLLING DOUGH: Keep unused dough refrigerated until ready to roll. Lightly flour rolling surface and rolling pin. (It is also helpful to pat flour on your hands.) For the most tender cookies, handle and reroll the dough as little as possible.
+ 3 Avoiding OVERBAKING: Cookies may be done even when they still look under-cooked. Watch for browning at the edges, which is a sign cookies are ready, and be brave enough to remove them when their allotted time is up.
+ 4 Preventing STICKING: To prevent sticking, spray cookie sheets with a light coat-

ing of cooking-oil spray, or line with parchment paper or greased aluminum foil.

+ 5 STORAGE: For best results, let cookies cool on cookie sheets until firm (usually 1 to 2 minutes), then transfer to wire racks to cool completely. Unless they are to be eaten right away, wrap cookies in plastic wrap, foil, or clear cellophane. Cookies may also be stored in airtight containers, such as cookie jars, metal tins, or resealable plastic bags. Stored this way, the cookies should remain tasty for up to a week. Crisp cookies should not be stored with soft cookies, or they will loose their crispness. A piece of bread in the cookie jar will help keep soft cookies soft. Unbaked cookie dough can be refrigerated for up to one week, or frozen for up to six weeks.

+ 6 INGREDIENTS: In the following recipes, unless otherwise specified, use *large* eggs, *all-purpose* flour, *unsalted* butter, and *granulated* sugar. For best results, and for ease in blending, butter and eggs should be brought to room temperature before mixing.

+ 7 PREPARATION: The cookies in the following recipes can be made using an elec-

tric mixer or by hand. When mixing by hand, be prepared to give your arm a thorough workout and take frequent breaks. *Superfine sugar* and a *wooden spoon* make mixing easier.

✦ 8 HELPFUL HINTS: Gather all ingredients before you start to work. This way, you won't have to stop to collect additional ingredients.

✦ 9 MEASUREMENTS: One stick of butter = ½ cup of butter = 8 tablespoons of butter = 4 ounces of butter.

✦ 10 HANGING ORNAMENTS: Cutout cookies make wonderful hanging ornaments. Simply make a hole in the cookie before baking. If the cookies are to be eaten eventually, wrap tightly in cellophane (colored cellophane tied with colorful ribbons is really festive), then hang, using ribbons, rubber bands, or hooks.

Extra-Special Ingredients

✦ 1 VANILLA SUGAR: Vanilla is a flavor that says *dessert*. Try making your own vanilla sugar—a common ingredient in European baking. Simply bury a whole vanilla bean in a jar of sugar and set aside for two weeks. Or finely chop a vanilla bean and add it to two cups of sugar. Use this wonderfully scented and flavored sugar as you would regular sugar.

✦ 2 CINNAMON SUGAR: Combine one cup of sugar with two teaspoons of cinnamon. Sprinkle over cookies for a sweet cinnamon-y treat.

• 3 COLORED SUGAR: Making your own colored sugar is easy and fun. Pour granulated sugar into a small bowl with a little food coloring—liquid, paste, or powder all work well. Work the colors in with your fingers. Apply the colored sugar to the cookies before baking, or sprinkle on top of wet royal icing.

• 4 ROYAL ICING: Royal icing is icing made with egg whites and powdered sugar. It can be flavored in as many ways as your imagination can devise! Add freshly squeezed fruit juices, such as lemon or orange, or extracts such as almond or vanilla. The icing can be colored with liquid, paste, or powdered colors—but apply these sparingly, using a toothpick, because a little color goes a long way. For added fun, put royal icing in several small bowls, and make each a different color. Icing can be applied to cookies with a spatula, a small paintbrush, a piping bag, or fingers. Powdered-sugar icing may be used in place of royal icing.

• 5 CHOCOLATE DRIZZLE: Semisweet, bittersweet, dark, milk, or white, melted chocolate is a wonderful and delicious way to decorate cookies. Drizzle over cookies, using a spoon, or allow to cool, and pipe, using a small pastry bag.

ANYTIME COOKIES

One day when Pooh Bear had nothing else to do, he thought he would do something, so he went round to Piglet's house to see what Piglet was doing.

—The House At Pooh Corner

✦ Plain & Simple Cookies ✦

¾ cup softened butter
  (1½ sticks)
⅔ cup sugar
3 teaspoons unsulfured
  molasses
1 teaspoon baking powder
2 cups flour
5 tablespoons milk
4 tablespoons finely
  chopped almonds
powdered sugar for rolling

Oven: 400° F

Beat butter and sugar together until fluffy.
Add molasses and baking powder, and mix
well. Slowly add flour, milk, and chopped
almonds and knead by hand to form a smooth
dough. Wrap and refrigerate until chilled,
about 2 hours.

Shape dough into finger-sized logs. Bake
on greased cookie sheets for 10 to 12 minutes,
until cookies are a light golden brown. While
still warm, roll cookies in powdered sugar.
Makes 3 dozen.

✦ Pecan Fingers ✦

¾ cup softened butter
  (1½ sticks)
6 tablespoons powdered
  sugar plus extra for
  rolling
2 cups flour
½ teaspoon salt
1½ teaspoons vanilla
  extract
1 tablespoon water
2 cups finely chopped
  pecans

OVEN: 300° F

Beat butter and powdered sugar together until fluffy. Slowly add flour, salt, vanilla extract, and water. Stir in pecans, then cover and refrigerate until chilled, about 4 hours.

Shape dough into finger-sized logs and bake on greased cookie sheets for 30 to 40 minutes. Cookies should be pale in color. Let cool slightly. While cookies are still warm, roll in powdered sugar. *Makes 2 dozen.*

✦ Chocolate Crisps ✦

1½ cups softened butter
   (3 sticks)
2¼ cups sugar
2 eggs
1 teaspoon vanilla extract
2½ cups flour
1¾ cups sifted cocoa
2½ teaspoons baking
   powder
¼ teaspoon salt

OVEN: 350° F

Beat butter and sugar together until fluffy.
Add eggs and vanilla extract, and mix well. In
another bowl, sift flour, cocoa, baking powder,
and salt together. Add to butter mixture,
mixing until all ingredients are thoroughly
combined. Divide dough in half, roll into logs,
wrap, and refrigerate until firm, about 2 hours.

Cut logs into ¼-inch-thick slices. Bake on
ungreased cookie sheets for 12 to 14 minutes.
Makes 5 dozen.

✦ Chocolate Butter Cookies ✦

¾ cup softened butter
  (1½ sticks)
½ cup sugar
1 egg yolk
1 teaspoon almond extract
1½ cups flour
¼ cup sifted cocoa
powdered sugar for dusting

Oven: 375° F

Beat butter and sugar together until fluffy. Add egg yolk and almond extract, and mix well. Slowly add flour and cocoa, and mix until all ingredients are thoroughly combined.

Shape dough into 1-inch balls with fingers, and bake on greased cookie sheets for 7 to 9 minutes. While still warm, roll cookies in powdered sugar. *Makes 3 dozen.*

✦ Brown-Sugar Chocolate-Chip Cookies ✦

2 cups softened butter
  (4 sticks)
1 cup sugar
3 cups dark brown sugar
4 eggs
2 teaspoons vanilla extract
3½ cups flour
1½ teaspoons salt
2 teaspoons baking soda
1⅓ cups semisweet
  chocolate chips

Oven: 375° F

Beat butter, sugar, and brown sugar together until fluffy. Add eggs and vanilla extract, and mix well. In another bowl, sift flour, salt, and baking soda, then add to butter mixture. Stir in chocolate chips. Drop batter by rounded tablespoons onto greased cookie sheets. Bake for 8 to 10 minutes. *Makes 2½ dozen.*

✦ Pecan Gingersnaps ✦

1 cup softened butter
  (2 sticks)
1¼ cups sugar
1 egg
½ cup unsulfured molasses
2½ cups flour
2½ teaspoons baking soda
½ teaspoon salt
2 tablespoons ground ginger
2 tablespoons coarsely
  chopped crystallized
  ginger
1¼ cups coarsely chopped
  pecans

OVEN: 325° F

Beat butter and sugar together until fluffy. Add the egg, then the molasses, and mix until all ingredients are thoroughly combined. In another bowl, sift flour, baking soda, salt, and ground ginger together, then slowly add to butter mixture. Mix well. Stir in crystallized ginger and chopped pecans. Roll dough into a log, wrap, and refrigerate until chilled, about 4 hours.

Cut log into ⅛-inch-thick slices. Bake on cookie sheets lined with parchment paper for 8 to 10 minutes until golden brown. (Cookies will spread a lot while cooking, so be sure to leave plenty of room between them.) *Makes 4 dozen.*

✦ Peanut Butter & Jelly Cookies ✦

½ cup creamy peanut
    butter
½ cup softened butter
    (1 stick)
2 tablespoons sugar
½ cup light brown sugar
1 teaspoon vanilla extract
1 egg
1 cup flour
½ teaspoon baking soda
pinch of salt
½ cup each of strawberry
    and apricot jam

OVEN: 375° F

Beat peanut butter, butter, sugar, and brown sugar together until smooth. Add vanilla extract and egg, and beat until fluffy. In another bowl, sift flour, baking soda, and salt together, and stir into peanut butter mixture until blended. Spoon heaping tablespoons of batter onto ungreased cookie sheets. Flatten slightly with hand and bake for 10 to 12 minutes. Remove cookie sheet from oven, and while cookies are still warm, press an indentation into the center of each cookie with thumb.

Heat jam in small saucepan until boiling. Allow to cool slightly, then spoon into the indentations in the middle of cookies. *Makes 2 dozen.*

✦ Brown-Sugar Nut Squares ✦

Cookie
1 cup flour
1 cup light brown sugar
½ cup vegetable shortening

Topping
2 tablespoons flour
¼ teaspoon salt
2 eggs
1 cup light brown sugar
1 teaspoon vanilla extract
½ cup coarsely chopped
 pecans, walnuts, or
 almonds

OVEN: 350° F

Mix flour and sugar, then cut shortening into mixture until crumbly. Press dough into 9 x 9-inch square pan that has been greased, lined with parchment paper, then greased again. Bake 15 minutes. Remove from oven and set aside.

Sift flour and salt together. Set aside. In another bowl, beat eggs till foamy, then add sugar and beat till fluffy. Add flour mixture and vanilla extract, and mix well. Stir in nuts. Spread topping over baked cookie, and return to oven for 30 minutes. Let cookie cool in pan, then remove and cut into 3-inch squares. *Makes 9 bars.*

✦ Piglet's Lemon Cookies ✦

½ cup softened butter
  (1 stick)
1 cup sugar
1 egg
½ teaspoon lemon extract
2 cups flour
½ teaspoon salt
1 teaspoon baking powder
¼ cup milk
1 egg, lightly beaten, for
  glaze
pink colored sugar for
  sprinkling

OVEN: 400° F

Beat butter and sugar together until fluffy. Add egg and lemon extract, and mix well. In another bowl, sift flour, salt, and baking powder together, and add little by little to butter mixture, alternating with milk. Mix until ingredients form a smooth dough. Chill thoroughly, at least 4 hours, or overnight.

Roll dough on lightly floured surface to ¼-inch thickness and cut with cookie cutters. Transfer to greased cookie sheets. Brush with beaten egg, and sprinkle with pink colored sugar. Bake for 7 to 10 minutes. *Makes 5 dozen.*

✦ Oatmeal Raisin Cookies ✦

¾ cup softened butter
(1½ sticks)

½ cup sugar

1 cup light or dark brown
sugar

1 teaspoon vanilla extract

1 egg

1¾ cups flour

¼ teaspoon ground cloves

½ teaspoon ground
cinnamon

1 teaspoon baking soda

2 cups rolled oats

1 cup raisins

OVEN: 375° F

Beat butter, sugar, and brown sugar together until fluffy. Add vanilla extract and egg, and mix well. In another bowl, sift flour, cloves, cinnamon, and baking soda together, then slowly add to butter mixture. Stir in oats and raisins. Drop by rounded teaspoons onto ungreased cookie sheets. Bake for 10 to 12 minutes, until edges are golden brown. *Makes 4 dozen.*

✦ Raisin Roll-ups ✦

Cookie Batter
½ cup shortening
1 cup sugar
½ cup light brown sugar
2 eggs
½ teaspoon vanilla extract
2 cups flour
½ teaspoon baking soda
½ teaspoon cinnamon
¼ teaspoon cream of tartar

Filling
1 cup chopped raisins
¼ cup sugar
¼ cup ground pecans
¼ cup water

Oven: 375° F

Beat shortening, sugar, and brown sugar together until blended. Add eggs and vanilla extract, and mix well. In another bowl, sift flour, baking soda, cinnamon, and cream of tartar together. Slowly add to shortening mixture. Blend to form a smooth dough. Wrap and refrigerate until chilled, about 4 hours.

Combine raisins, sugar, pecans, and water in small saucepan, and bring to a boil. Reduce heat and simmer, stirring constantly for about 3 minutes, or until water is absorbed and mixture is thick. Allow to cool.

On a lightly floured surface, roll chilled dough to ¼-inch thickness. Trim edges to form a rectangle, then spread filling over dough. Roll up jelly-roll style. Cover and refrigerate until firm, about 2 hours.

Cut roll into ¼-inch-thick slices, and bake on greased cookie sheets for 6 to 8 minutes, until cookies are light brown. *Makes 3 dozen.*

✦ Expotition Cookies ✦

½ cup softened butter
  (1 stick)
1 cup sugar
1 cup unsulfured molasses
1 teaspoon baking soda
3½ cups flour
2 teaspoons ground ginger
½ teaspoon nutmeg
½ teaspoon allspice
½ teaspoon ground cloves
pinch of salt
1 tablespoon finely chopped
  crystallized ginger

Oven: 375° F

Beat butter and sugar together until fluffy. In another bowl, combine molasses and baking soda. Add molasses mixture to butter mixture, and mix until all ingredients are thoroughly combined. In another bowl, sift flour, spices, and salt together, then slowly add to butter mixture. Stir in crystallized ginger. Wrap and refrigerate dough until chilled, about 4 hours.

Divide dough in half. Working with one half at a time, roll on lightly floured surface to ¼-inch thickness. Cut, using 3- or 4-inch round cookie cutters. Bake on greased cookie sheets for 10 to 12 minutes. *Makes 2 dozen.*

✦ Cinnamon Sugar Slices ✦

½ cup softened butter
  (1 stick)
½ cup shortening
½ cup sugar
½ cup light brown sugar
1 egg
½ teaspoon vanilla extract
2½ cups flour
1 teaspoon cinnamon
½ teaspoon baking soda
cinnamon sugar for
  sprinkling

OVEN: 350° F

Beat butter, shortening, sugar, and brown
sugar together until fluffy. Add egg and vanilla
extract, and mix well. In another bowl, sift
flour, cinnamon, and baking soda together, and
slowly add to butter mixture. Mix until
thoroughly combined. Shape into log, wrap,
and refrigerate until chilled, about 4 hours.

Cut log into ¼-inch-thick slices and sprinkle
with cinnamon sugar. Bake on ungreased cookie
sheets for 8 minutes, until edges are golden
brown. *Makes 4 dozen.*

COOKIES FOR COMPANY

"Aha!" said Pooh. (Rum-tum-tiddle-um-tum.) *"If I know anything about anything, that hole means Rabbit,"* he said, *"and Rabbit means Company,"* he said, *"and Company means Food."*

—Winnie-the-Pooh

✦ Coffee Cookies ✦

1 cup softened butter
  (2 sticks)
1¼ cups sugar
½ cup instant coffee
2½ tablespoons vanilla
  extract
3 egg yolks
2½ cups plus
  3 tablespoons cake flour

Oven: 350° F

Beat butter and sugar together until fluffy. Set aside. In a separate bowl, mix coffee, vanilla extract, and egg yolks. Add to butter mixture and beat. Slowly add the flour and continue to beat until thoroughly blended. Drop by rounded teaspoons onto greased cookie sheets and bake for 15 to 18 minutes. *Makes 3 dozen.*

✦ Lemon-Glazed Tea Cookies ✦

Cookies
⅓ cup milk
2 teaspoons lemon juice
½ cup softened butter
   (1 stick)
¾ cup sugar
1 egg
1¾ cups flour
1 teaspoon baking powder
¼ teaspoon baking soda
1 teaspoon lemon zest

Glaze
¼ cup sugar
2 tablespoons lemon juice

Oven: 350° F

Stir 2 teaspoons of milk into lemon juice. Set aside. Beat butter and sugar together until fluffy. Add egg, lemon juice–milk mixture, and remaining milk, and mix well. In another bowl, sift flour, baking powder, and baking soda together, and slowly add to butter mixture. Stir in lemon zest. Drop by rounded teaspoons onto ungreased cookie sheets and bake for 10 to 12 minutes. Edges should be lightly brown. Mix lemon juice and sugar for glaze. Allow cookies to cool, then brush with lemon-sugar glaze mixture. *Makes 3 dozen.*

✦ Peanut-Butter Cutouts ✦

4 cups flour
¼ teaspoon salt
1 tablespoon baking powder
1 cup creamy peanut butter
1 cup softened butter
  (2 sticks)
1 cup dark brown sugar
2 eggs
⅔ cup corn syrup

Oven: 325° F

Sift flour, salt, and baking powder together. Set aside. In another bowl, beat peanut butter, butter, brown sugar, eggs, and corn syrup until smooth. Slowly add flour mixture, and blend to form a smooth dough. Wrap and refrigerate until chilled, about 2 hours.

Divide dough in half. Working with one half at a time, roll on lightly floured surface to ⅛-inch thickness for thin cookies, ¼-inch for thicker, softer cookies. Cut with cookie cutters. Bake on ungreased cookie sheets for 8 to 10 minutes. Decorate with piped chocolate, royal icing, or powdered-sugar icing, or enjoy plain. *Makes 3 dozen.*

✦ Cream-Cheese Cookies ✦

¼ cup softened butter
  (1½ sticks)
½ cup softened cream
  cheese
¾ cup sugar
1 egg
1 teaspoon vanilla extract
2 cups flour
¼ teaspoon baking soda
¼ teaspoon salt
1 egg white, lightly beaten
colored sugar for decorating

OVEN: 350° F

Beat butter, cream cheese, and sugar together until fluffy. Add egg and vanilla extract, and mix well. In another bowl, sift flour, baking soda, and salt together, and stir into butter mixture. Wrap and refrigerate until chilled, about 4 hours.

Divide dough into quarters. Working with one section at a time, roll on well-floured surface to ¼-inch thickness. Cut, using cookie cutters. Brush tops with egg white and sprinkle with colored sugar. Bake on greased cookie sheets for 8 to 10 minutes. *Makes 3 dozen.*

✦ Sables ✦

¾ cup butter (1½ sticks)
⅔ cup sugar
2 egg yolks
1 teaspoon vanilla extract
2 cups flour
1 beaten egg for glaze
granulated or colored sugar
   for sprinkling

OVEN: 350° F

Beat butter and sugar together until fluffy.
Add egg yolks and vanilla extract, and mix
well. Slowly add flour and blend until dough
is smooth, scraping sides of bowl often. Divide
dough in half and refrigerate until chilled,
about 4 hours.

Working with one section of dough at a
time, roll on a well-floured surface to ⅛-inch
thickness for crisp cookies, ¼-inch for soft
cookies. Using a cookie cutter with fluted edges,
cut into rounds and transfer to a greased cookie
sheet. Using a pastry brush, brush top with
beaten egg and sprinkle with sugar. Bake for 8
to 10 minutes, or until cookies are a pale golden
color. *Makes 3 dozen.*

✦ Chewy Chocolate-Chunk Cookies ✦

1 cup softened butter
(2 sticks)
1 cup sugar
1 cup light brown sugar
2 eggs
2 teaspoons vanilla extract
2 cups flour
¾ cup sifted cocoa
2 teaspoons baking powder
1 teaspoon salt
⅔ cup coarsely chopped
bittersweet chocolate

OVEN: 325° F

Beat butter, sugar, and brown sugar together until fluffy. Add eggs and vanilla extract, and mix well. In a separate bowl, sift flour, cocoa, baking powder, and salt together, and stir into butter mixture. Add chocolate and mix. Line cookie sheets with parchment paper. Drop batter by rounded tablespoons onto cookie sheets and bake for 8 to 10 minutes. *Makes 4 dozen.*

✦ Chocolate Orange Fingers ✦

Cookies

1 cup softened butter
  (2 sticks)
¼ cup powdered sugar
1 tablespoon orange extract
2 cups flour
2 tablespoons cornstarch
¼ teaspoon salt

OVEN: 350° F

Chocolate

⅔ cup finely chopped
  semisweet or bittersweet
  chocolate
1 teaspoon vegetable
  shortening

Beat butter and powdered sugar together until fluffy. Add orange extract. In another bowl, sift flour, cornstarch, and salt together, then stir into butter mixture. Mix until dough is smooth, adding a little water if necessary. Form dough into 2-inch fingers. Bake 15 minutes on ungreased cookie sheets. Set aside to cool.

Melt chocolate and shortening in a double boiler, or in a bowl over simmering water. Dip one end of cooled cookie into chocolate. Dry on waxed paper. *Makes 5 dozen.*

✦ Madeleines ✦

½ cup butter (1 stick)
4 eggs at room temperature
⅓ teaspoon salt
⅔ cup sugar
1 teaspoon vanilla extract
1 cup flour
powdered sugar for dusting

OVEN: 375° F

Butter and flour 2 madeleine tins. Melt butter and set aside to cool. Beat eggs and salt, slowly adding sugar until mixture stands in stiff peaks. Add vanilla extract. Slowly sift flour into mixture, and fold until thoroughly blended. Add cooled butter to mixture, pouring slowly, but folding as quickly as possible. Fill tins almost to the top, and bake for 8 to 10 minutes. Remove from tins immediately. Once cookies have cooled, dust with powdered sugar. *Makes 3 dozen.*

✦ Christopher Robin's Button Cookies ✦

1 cup softened butter
  (2 sticks)
½ cup sugar
⅔ cup light brown sugar
1 teaspoon vanilla or
  almond extract
1 egg
2½ cups flour
1 teaspoon salt

Oven: 350° F

Beat butter, sugar, and brown sugar together until fluffy. Add extract and egg, and mix well. Add flour and salt, and mix until all ingredients are thoroughly combined. Wrap and refrigerate until chilled, about 2 hours.

Line cookie sheets with parchment paper. Roll dough into a log and slice into ¼-inch rounds. Using a toothpick, press four decorative holes, arranged as on a button, into tops of cookies. Bake for 15 to 20 minutes, or until cookies are golden brown. *Makes 3 ½ dozen.*

✦ Tigger-Striped Shortbread ✦

1¼ cups flour
¼ cup plus 1 tablespoon
  sugar
⅛ teaspoon salt
½ cup cold butter (1 stick),
  cut into small pieces
chocolate drizzle

Oven: 325° F

Lightly butter a 9-inch pie pan. Sift flour, sugar, and salt together. Using your fingers, work the butter into the flour mixture until crumbly. Gently knead the dough together. Press dough into prepared pan, evenly covering the bottom. Prick with a fork, and bake 30 to 35 minutes. Shortbread should be lightly brown around edges. Cut into 8 wedges while still warm and let cool in pan. Once cookies have cooled, remove from pan, and use chocolate drizzle to form Tigger's stripes. *Makes 8 wedges.*

✦ Piglet's Pine-Nut Cutouts ✦

½ cup softened butter
  (1 stick)
½ cup sugar
1 teaspoon vanilla extract
¼ cup hot water
2 cups flour
½ teaspoon salt
1 egg white plus one
  teaspoon water,
  lightly beaten
⅔ cup pine nuts
sugar for sprinkling

Oven: 375° F

Beat butter and sugar together until fluffy.
Gradually beat in vanilla extract and hot water.
In another bowl, sift flour and salt together,
then stir into butter mixture. Wrap and refrigerate until chilled, about 1 hour.

On a lightly floured surface, roll dough to
¼-inch thickness. Cut, using variously shaped
cookie cutters. Transfer to greased cookie sheets.
Brush tops with egg white, and sprinkle with
pine nuts and sugar. Bake for 15 minutes, or
until cookies are light brown. *Makes 2 dozen.*

✦ Rainy-Day Jam Cookies ✦

½ cup plus 3 tablespoons
   of butter
½ cup sugar
2 egg yolks
1 teaspoon vanilla extract
1½ cups flour
¼ cup each of assorted
   jams or preserves, such as
   strawberry, apricot,
   peach, or blueberry

OVEN: 375° F

Beat butter and sugar together until fluffy.
Add egg yolks and vanilla extract, and mix
well. Slowly add flour and beat until
thoroughly combined. Cover dough and
refrigerate until chilled, about 4 hours.

Using your hands, roll dough into 1-inch
balls. Place on greased cookie sheets, flatten
slightly with hand, and press an indentation
into the center of each cookie with thumb.
Bake 10 to 12 minutes. Remove and set aside
to cool. Heat jams or preserves in small
saucepan until boiling. Remove from heat
and allow jam to cool slightly. Once cookies
have cooled, fill the centers with the warm
jam. *Makes 3 ½ dozen.*

HONEY-POT COOKIES

Pooh said good-bye affectionately to his fourteen pots of honey, and hoped they were fifteen; and he and Rabbit went out into the Forest.

—The House At Pooh Corner

✦ Honey-Pecan Shortbread ✦

1 cup softened butter
  (2 sticks)
⅓ cup honey
1½ teaspoons vanilla extract
2½ cups flour
½ cup chopped pecans

OVEN: 300° F

Beat butter, honey, and vanilla extract together until fluffy. Slowly add flour and mix until dough is smooth. Knead in pecans. Press dough into shortbread mold. Score surface with knife to form wedges. Bake for 35 to 40 minutes. Shortbread will be pale. Allow to cool in pan for 10 minutes, then remove and cut into wedges. *Makes 2 dozen.*

✦ Granola-Honey Squares ✦

1 cup quick-rolled oats
½ cup flour
1 cup granola
1 cup coarsely chopped
   pecans or walnuts
½ cup raisins
1 egg
⅓ cup honey
⅓ cup canola oil
½ teaspoon cinnamon
¼ cup light brown sugar

Oven: 325° F

Combine oats, flour, granola, nuts, and raisins. In a separate bowl, beat egg until foamy, and stir into oat mixture. Add honey, oil, cinnamon, and brown sugar. Stir until thoroughly mixed. Line an 8 x 8 x 2-inch baking pan with foil, then grease foil. Press dough into pan and bake 30 to 35 minutes until golden brown. Cool and cut into 2-inch squares. *Makes 16 squares.*

✦ Honey Madeleines ✦

¾ cup plus 1 tablespoon
  butter
½ cup plus 1 tablespoon
  flour
1⅔ cups powdered sugar
½ cup ground almonds
6 egg whites
2 tablespoons honey
powdered sugar for dusting

OVEN: 375° F

Melt one tablespoon of butter and, using a pastry brush, thoroughly coat two madeleine tins. Dust lightly with flour. Set aside. Heat remaining butter over moderately high heat until it begins to brown, about 5 minutes. Transfer butter to bowl and set aside to cool. Sift flour and sugar together, then stir in ground almonds. In a separate bowl, beat egg whites until frothy. Stir egg whites into flour mixture, then whisk in butter and honey. Spoon batter into prepared tins, filling almost to the top. Refrigerate for 1 hour.

Bake for 12 to 15 minutes, until cookies are lightly golden. Remove from tins immediately, using a knife if necessary. Cool on racks, and dust with powdered sugar. *Makes 2½ dozen.*

✦ Chocolate Honey Madeleines ✦

¾ cup plus 1 tablespoon
  butter
½ cup finely grated
  bittersweet chocolate
½ cup plus 1 tablespoon
  flour
1⅔ cups powdered sugar
½ cup ground almonds
6 egg whites
1 tablespoon honey

Oven: 375° F

Melt one tablespoon butter and, using a pastry brush, thoroughly coat two madeleine tins. Dust lightly with flour. Set aside. Heat remaining butter over moderately high heat until it begins to brown, about 5 minutes. Transfer butter to bowl and set aside to cool. Melt chocolate in a double boiler, or in a bowl over simmering water. Set aside to cool. Sift flour and sugar together, then stir in ground almonds. In a separate bowl, beat egg whites until frothy, then stir into flour mixture. Whisk in butter and honey, then add melted chocolate. Whisk until thoroughly combined. Spoon batter into tins, filling almost to the top. Refrigerate for 1 hour.

Bake for 12 to 15 minutes. Cookies should be springy to the touch. Remove from tins immediately, using a knife if necessary. Cool on racks. *Makes 2½ dozen.*

✦ Chocolate-Chip Honey Cookies ✦

½ cup softened butter
(1 stick)
½ teaspoon vanilla extract
½ cup honey
1 egg
1¼ cups flour
½ teaspoon baking soda
½ teaspoon salt
¾ cup chopped pecans
or walnuts
1 cup semisweet chocolate
chips

OVEN: 375° F

Cream butter, then mix in vanilla extract and honey. Add egg and mix well. In another bowl, sift flour, baking soda, and salt together, and add to batter mixture. Stir in nuts and chocolate chips. Line cookie sheets with parchment paper. Drop batter by rounded tablespoons onto cookie sheets. Bake for 13 to 15 minutes until golden brown. *Makes 2 dozen.*

✦ Honey Carrot Cookies ✦

½ cup softened butter
(1 stick)
1 cup sugar
2 eggs
3 tablespoons honey
1 teaspoon vanilla extract
2¼ cups flour
2 teaspoons baking soda
pinch of salt
½ teaspoon nutmeg
½ cup shredded carrots
granulated sugar

Oven: 325° F

Beat butter and sugar together until fluffy. Add eggs, honey, and vanilla extract, and beat until thoroughly blended. In another bowl, sift flour, baking soda, salt, and nutmeg together, and slowly add to butter mixture. Stir in carrots. Flour hands and shape batter into 1-inch balls. Sprinkle with granulated sugar. Bake on ungreased cookie sheets for 12 to 15 minutes, or until edges are golden brown. *Makes 3 dozen.*

✦ Honey Lace Sandwiches ✦

3 cups sliced almonds
¼ cup softened butter
  (½ stick)
⅔ cup heavy cream
1 cup sugar
½ cup honey
½ cup flour
½ cup finely chopped
  crystallized ginger
1 teaspoon vanilla extract
½ teaspoon ground
  cinnamon
8 ounces bittersweet
  chocolate for icing

OVEN: 325° F

Coarsely chop 2 cups of almonds; grind remainder in blender or food processor. Heat butter, cream, sugar, and honey in small saucepan and bring to a boil. Continue cooking until mixture reaches 238° F on a candy thermometer. Stir in flour, crystallized ginger, vanilla extract, and cinnamon, and let mixture cool.

Line cookie sheets with parchment paper, then brush with melted butter. Drop cooled mixture by teaspoons onto cookie sheets. Make sure to leave at least 3 inches between cookies. Bake for 12 minutes, or until cookies are golden in color. Allow to cool. Meanwhile, melt chocolate in a bowl over hot water. Coat one side of cooled cookie with chocolate and top with another cookie before chocolate has time to set. *Makes 2 dozen.*

HOLIDAY COOKIES
AND ICINGS

One fine winter's day when Piglet was brushing away the snow in front of his house, he happened to look up, and there was Winnie-the-Pooh.

—Winnie-the-Pooh

✦ Snowballs ✦

1 cup softened butter
  (2 sticks)
⅓ cup sugar
1 teaspoon vanilla extract
2 egg yolks
zest of two oranges
¼ cup orange juice
3 cups flour
1 cup ground almonds
powdered sugar for dusting

Oven: 350° F

Beat butter and sugar together until fluffy. Add vanilla extract, egg yolks, orange zest, and orange juice, and beat until thoroughly combined. Add flour, then stir in ground nuts. Wrap and refrigerate dough until chilled, about 1 hour.

Line cookie sheets with parchment paper. On lightly floured surface, roll dough into 1-inch balls. Bake for 8 to 10 minutes. While cookies are still warm, roll in powdered sugar. Roll again once cookies have cooled. *Makes 3 dozen.*

✦ Maple Syrup Cookies ✦

1 cup softened butter
  (2 sticks)
¼ cup sugar
½ cup dark brown sugar
¼ cup maple syrup
¼ cup unsulfured molasses
1 egg
2 cups flour
¼ teaspoon baking soda
1¼ teaspoons ground
  ginger
½ teaspoon allspice
½ teaspoon cinnamon
½ cup raisins
1½ cups chopped nuts
pinch of salt
cinnamon sugar, for
  sprinkling

OVEN: 375° F

Beat butter, sugar, and brown sugar together
until fluffy. Add syrup, molasses, and egg.
Mix thoroughly. Stir in flour, baking soda,
spices, raisins, nuts, and salt. Drop by rounded
tablespoons onto greased cookie sheets. Sprinkle
with cinnamon sugar. Bake 12 minutes, until
edges are brown. *Makes 3 dozen.*

✦ Gingerbread Cookies ✦

½ cup softened butter
  (1 stick)
½ cup light brown sugar
1 egg
¾ cup unsulfured molasses
3 cups flour
¼ teaspoon salt
1 teaspoon ground ginger
1 teaspoon cinnamon
½ teaspoon ground cloves
½ teaspoon ground
  nutmeg
½ teaspoon baking soda

OVEN: 350° F

Beat butter and brown sugar together until fluffy. Add egg and molasses, and mix well. In another bowl, sift flour, salt, spices, and baking soda together. Stir into butter mixture. Mix until all ingredients are thoroughly combined. Wrap and refrigerate until chilled, about 4 hours.

On well-floured surface, roll dough to ¼-inch thickness and cut with cookie cutters. Bake on greased cookie sheets for 8 minutes. Cool completely, then decorate with royal icing or powdered-sugar icing. *Makes 2 dozen.*

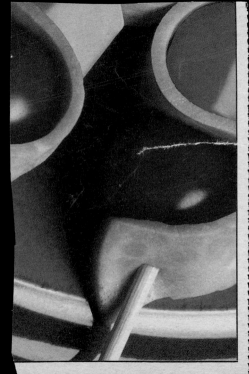

Peanut Blossoms

48 HERSHEY'S KISSES® Milk Chocolates
1/2 cup shortening
3/4 cup REESE'S® Creamy or Crunchy Peanut Butter
1/3 cup granulated sugar
1/3 cup packed light brown sugar

1 egg
2 tablespoons milk
1 teaspoon vanilla extract
1 1/2 cups all-purpose flour
1 teaspoon baking soda
1/2 teaspoon salt
Granulated sugar

1. Heat oven to 375° F. Remove wrappers from KISSES.™

2. In large bowl, beat shortening and peanut butter until well blended. Add 1/3 cup granulated sugar and brown sugar; beat until light and fluffy. Add egg, milk and vanilla; beat well. Stir together flour, baking soda and salt; gradually add to peanut butter mixture. Shape dough into 1-inch balls. Roll in granulated sugar; place on ungreased cookie sheet.

3. Bake 8 to 10 minutes or until lightly browned. Immediately place KISS™ on top of each cookie, pressing down so cookie cracks around edges. Remove from cookie sheet to wire rack. Cool completely. About 4 dozen cookies.

✦ Vanilla Sugar Cutouts ✦

1 cup softened butter
  (2 sticks)
2 cups sugar or vanilla
  sugar
2 eggs
1 teaspoon vanilla extract
4½ cups flour
1 teaspoon salt
4 teaspoons baking powder
½ cup milk

OVEN: 375° F

Beat butter and sugar together until fluffy.
Add eggs and vanilla extract, and mix well. In
another bowl, sift flour, salt, and baking powder
together. Alternating between milk and dry
ingredients, blend into butter mixture. Wrap
and refrigerate until chilled, about 4 hours.

On lightly floured surface, roll dough to
¼-inch thickness and cut, using variously
shaped cookie cutters. Bake for 8 to 10 minutes.
Cookies will be pale. When cool, ice with royal
icing or powdered-sugar icing. *Makes 3 dozen.*

✦ Chocolate Sugar Cutouts ✦

½ cup softened butter
  (1 stick)
⅔ cup sugar
⅓ cup cocoa powder
1 egg
1½ cups flour
½ teaspoon baking powder
¼ teaspoon salt

Oven: 350° F

Beat butter and sugar together until fluffy. Add cocoa and mix well. Add egg, and beat until thoroughly combined. In another bowl, sift flour, baking powder, and salt together, and slowly add to butter mixture. Mix until all ingredients are blended. Wrap and refrigerate until chilled, about 4 hours.

On a lightly floured surface, roll dough to ¼-inch thickness. Cut with cookie cutters and transfer to ungreased cookie sheets. Bake for 12 to 15 minutes. Ice with royal icing or powdered-sugar icing, or decorate with chocolate drizzle. *Makes 2½ dozen.*

✦ Pumpkin Squares ✦

2 cups flour
1½ cups sugar
2 teaspoons baking powder
1 teaspoon baking soda
2 teaspoons ground
   cinnamon
¼ teaspoon salt
¼ teaspoon ground cloves
4 eggs
1 15-ounce can of
   pumpkin puree
1 cup vegetable oil
powdered sugar for dusting

OVEN: 350° F

Combine flour, sugar, baking powder, baking soda, cinnamon, salt, and cloves. Mix well. In another bowl, beat eggs until foamy, then add them to flour mixture. Stir in pumpkin puree and oil. Mix until all ingredients are thoroughly combined. Spread batter into an ungreased large shallow baking or jelly-roll pan, preferably 15 x 10 x 1 inch. If necessary, use two smaller pans. Bake for 25 to 30 minutes, or until toothpick inserted into center comes out clean. Cool in pan and cut into squares. Dust with powdered sugar or frost with cream-cheese frosting. *Makes 4 dozen.*

✦ Banana Spice Cookies ✦

½ cup softened butter
  (1 stick)
1 cup sugar
2 eggs
1 teaspoon vanilla extract
2¼ cups flour
½ teaspoon cinnamon
⅛ teaspoon ground cloves
¼ teaspoon baking soda
3 mashed bananas
½ cup chopped pecans
  or walnuts
powdered sugar for dusting

Oven: 350° F

Beat butter and sugar together until fluffy.
Add eggs and vanilla extract, and mix well.
In another bowl, sift flour, spices, and baking
soda together, and stir into butter mixture.
Add bananas and nuts, and mix well. Drop by
rounded teaspoons onto greased cookie sheets
and bake for 8 to 10 minutes, or until edges are
lightly brown. Dust with powdered sugar or ice
with cream-cheese frosting. *Makes 3 dozen.*

✦ Ginger Cookie Cutouts ✦

¾ cup softened butter
   (1½ sticks)
1½ cups sugar
1 egg
¾ teaspoon vanilla extract
¼ cup unsulfured molasses
2½ cups flour
¾ teaspoon ground ginger
1 teaspoon cinnamon
¼ teaspoon baking powder
⅓ teaspoon salt

OVEN: 350° F

Beat butter and sugar together until fluffy. Add egg and vanilla extract, and beat until thoroughly combined. Stir in molasses. In another bowl, sift flour, ginger, cinnamon, baking powder, and salt together, and stir into butter mixture. Mix well to form a smooth dough. Wrap and refrigerate dough until chilled, about 4 hours.

Roll dough on lightly floured surface to ¼-inch thickness and cut, using cookie cutters. Bake on ungreased cookie sheets for 12 to 15 minutes, or until edges start to brown. Decorate with royal icing or powdered-sugar icing, or enjoy plain. *Makes 3 dozen.*

✦ Old-Fashioned Molasses Cookies ✦

¾ cup softened butter
   (1½ sticks)
1 cup sugar
⅓ cup unsulfured molasses
1 egg
3 tablespoons milk
2 cups flour
½ teaspoon ground cloves
½ teaspoon cinnamon
½ teaspoon ginger
½ teaspoon baking soda
pinch of salt
sugar for rolling

OVEN: 350° F

Beat butter and sugar together until fluffy. Add molasses, egg, and milk, and mix well. In another bowl, sift flour, spices, baking soda, and salt together, and add to butter mixture. Mix until all ingredients are thoroughly combined. Wrap and refrigerate dough until chilled, about 4 hours.

Using hands, shape dough into 1-inch balls. Roll in sugar and bake on ungreased cookie sheets for 8 to 12 minutes. *Makes 4 dozen.*

✦ Chocolate-Chip Macaroons ✦

⅔ cup sweetened
   condensed milk
1 teaspoon vanilla extract
2½ cups flaked coconut
⅔ cup mini semisweet
   chocolate chips

OVEN: 350° F

Combine all ingredients in medium bowl and mix until thoroughly blended. Drop by rounded teaspoons onto greased cookie sheets and bake for 10 to 12 minutes. Cookies will be light brown. *Makes 3 dozen.*

✦ Cream-Cheese Frosting ✦

6 ounces soft cream cheese
½ cup softened butter
  (1 stick)
2 teaspoons vanilla extract
4½ cups sifted powdered
  sugar

Beat cream cheese, butter, and vanilla extract together until fluffy. Slowly beat in 2 cups of powdered sugar. Mix well. Add remaining sugar and mix until frosting is of spreading consistency. Add more sugar if frosting is too thin. Refrigerate cookies after frosting. *Makes 4 cups.*

✦ Royal Icing ✦

1 egg white
1 cup powdered sugar
½ teaspoon vanilla or
    almond extract or fresh
    lemon juice
pinch of cream of tartar
2 drops glycerin (to make
    the icing shiny)
food coloring (optional)

Combine and beat all ingredients until icing holds its shape in sharp peaks when beater is lifted. Add a few drops of water if icing is too thick; add more sugar if it is too thin. Stir in food coloring. Spread on cookies, or pipe, using pastry bag. *Makes 1 cup.*

✦ Meringue-Powder Royal Icing ✦

1½ tablespoons meringue
   powder
2 cups powdered sugar
3 tablespoons warm water
1 teaspoon vanilla extract

Mix all ingredients together and blend until desired consistency is formed: stiff peaks for piping, soft peaks for spreading. Add food coloring if desired. *Makes 2 cups.*

✦ Powdered-Sugar Icing ✦

2 cups powdered sugar
½ teaspoon vanilla extract
2 tablespoons milk or
   orange juice

In a medium bowl, stir all ingredients together until smooth. Use additional milk or orange juice if necessary. Stir in food coloring if desired. Spread over cookies. *Makes 2 cups.*

✦ Chocolate Drizzle ✦

4 ounces of your favorite chocolate

Chop chocolate into small pieces. Melt chocolate in a double boiler, or place in a small bowl over a pan of simmering water. Once chocolate is completely melted, drizzle over the tops of cookies, using a spoon, or pipe, using a pastry bag with a small tip. Cookies may also be dipped and placed on waxed or parchment paper to dry. Cookies will set faster if placed in the refrigerator for five minutes.

"You're the Best Bear in All the World," said Christopher Robin soothingly.

"Am I?" said Pooh hopefully. And then he brightened up suddenly.

"Anyhow," he said, *"it is nearly Luncheon Time."*

So he went home for it.   —Winnie-the-Pooh

INDEX